ANDY WARHOL
POP ART PAINTER

BY SUSAN GOLDMAN RUBIN

ABRAMS BOOKS FOR YOUNG READERS
NEW YORK

TO MICHAEL AND *OUR* ANDY

ACKNOWLEDGMENTS

I want to thank my editor, Howard Reeves, for producing this book. Working with him has been a great pleasure from start to finish. With Howard's encouragement I contacted various people who knew Andy Warhol: his nephew James Warhola; artists Len Kessler and Philip Pearlstein; his second assistant Nathan Gluck; the executive editor of his magazine, *Interview*, Bob Colacello; and art historian Tom Sokolowski, director of the Andy Warhol Museum. I am grateful to them all for sharing their reminiscences of Andy Warhol. Thanks also to Matt Wrbican, assistant archivist at the Andy Warhol Museum. A big thank-you to Celina Carvalho for her wonderful design, and Leslie Dutcher at Abrams for diligently acquiring permissions to reproduce the art in this book. And a special thank you to my writer friends, "Lunch Bunch" and the Thursday night group, for their critiques, support, and interest.

As always I express my deep gratitude to George Nicholson—agent, friend, and mentor—who believes in the value of art books for children as I do. And last, a word of thanks to his trusty assistant, Thaddeus Bower.

Design by Celina Carvalho
Production Manager: Alexis Mentor
Photo Research: Leslie Dutcher

Library of Congress Cataloging-in-Publication Data:
Rubin, Susan Goldman.
Andy Warhol : pop art painter / Susan Goldman Rubin.
p. cm.
1. Warhol, Andy, 1928– 2. Artists—United States—Biography. 3. Pop art—United States.
I. Title: Pop art painter. II. Title.

ISBN 10: 0-8109-5477-X
ISBN 13: 978-0-8109-5477-9
N6537.W28R83 2005
700'.92—dc22
2005013238

Text copyright © 2006 Susan Goldman Rubin
See page 47 for illustration credits

Published in 2006 by Abrams Books for Young Readers, an imprint of Harry N. Abrams, Inc.

Printed and bound in Singapore
10 9 8 7 6 5 4 3 2 1

harry n. abrams, inc.
a subsidiary of La Martinière Groupe
115 West 18th Street, New York, NY 10011
www.hnabooks.com

CONTENTS

BIOGRAPHY 4

TIME LINE 34

GLOSSARY 43

SOURCE NOTES 44

REFERENCES AND RESOURCES 46

ILLUSTRATION CREDITS 47

AUTHOR'S NOTE 48

SOME MUSEUMS WHERE YOU

WILL FIND WORK BY ANDY WARHOL 48

▼ *Andy Warhol (right) with his Brother Paul*, 1942

As a child Andy Warhol liked to draw. "I drew pictures, so Andy made pictures when he was a little boy," recalled his mother, Julia. "He made very nice pictures. We made pictures together." When Andy and his older brothers, John and Paul, got rowdy, she brought them into the kitchen, gave them paper and crayons, and offered a prize for the best drawing. Andy always won. The prize was a big Hershey bar and he adored chocolate.

"He just loved to draw with crayons," remembered John. The boys sat and drew at the kitchen table where they ate their meals. "I used to have the same lunch every day for twenty years," Andy remembered. "Soup and a sandwich." Campbell's soup. "Many an afternoon Mom would open a can of Campbell's tomato soup for me because that's all we could afford. I love it to this day." Campbell's soup had a great effect on Andy's art. The soup can would become the subject of paintings that would one day make him famous.

"I USED TO HAVE THE SAME LUNCH EVERY DAY FOR TWENTY YEARS," ANDY REMEMBERED. "SOUP AND A SANDWICH."

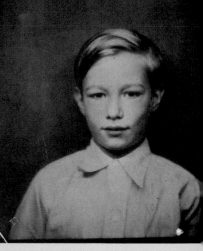

and danced and did all of Rusyn craft traditions," recalled her grandson James Warhola.

When Andy was three years old, his father, Ondrej, a construction worker, lost his job and the family moved to a small apartment. Julia helped out by cleaning houses and making crepe paper flowers arranged in empty food cans. She cut the sides of the cans into the shape of stems and attached the flowers to form bouquets. Then she sold her handicrafts door-to-door. Andy always remembered these "flower sculptures." He said, "The tin flowers she made out of those fruit tins, that's the reason why I did my first tin-can paintings . . . My mother always had lots of cans around, including the soup cans. She was . . . a real good and correct artist."

At public school Andy's talent for drawing was noticed. "He was a good little artist in second grade," said one of his teachers. Andy especially loved coloring books and comic books. He also loved movies and collected pictures of movie stars. His older brothers helped him write letters requesting autographed photos. His favorite movie star was Shirley Temple, a child who danced and sang on the screen. Once Andy sent a dime to Shirley Temple's fan club and received a picture of her, which he treasured. Years later he said, "I never wanted to be a painter; I wanted to be a tap dancer."

Andy's interest in photography led his brother Paul to buy him his first camera, a small Brownie. Paul taught him how to use it and how to develop pictures in a darkroom they built in their old fruit cellar. Andy took pictures of the rabbit hutch in their backyard and daisies in his flower garden. His garden won a prize for the best in the neighborhood.

Andy, the youngest of three brothers, grew up in Pittsburgh, Pennsylvania. He was born on August 6, 1928, and named for his father, Ondrej (Andrew) Warhola. Andy's parents had met and married in a Carpatho-Rusyn village in Slovakia, and soon after emigrated to America. At home in Pittsburgh, they continued to speak their native Carpatho-Rusyn language. Andy and his brothers understood it, but they spoke to their parents in English. Their mother, Julia Zavacky Warhola, clung to many old-world customs such as wearing a *bubushka*, a kerchief, on her head. She also told the boys stories about the "old country" and the year when she and one of her sisters had traveled around the countryside singing with the Gypsies. Her side of the family was musical and artistic. "They all sang

"A MORE TALENTED PERSON THAN ANDY WARHOL I NEVER KNEW."

Dick Tracy, 1960. ▶
Casein and crayon on canvas,
48 x 33 7/8 in.

Leonardo da Vinci. *The Last Supper,* 1494–1498.
Tempera and oil on two layers of prepared surface: lead white and a
coarser coating of calcium carbonite, laid over plaster, 179 3/8 x 343 1/4 in. ▼

When Andy was eight he came down with rheumatic fever. The doctor ordered bed rest. When Andy went back to school ten weeks later, he still felt sick. The condition made him shake and turn very pale. Andy had to stay in bed again—this time for months! He kept busy with comics, paper dolls, and coloring books. His mother read *Dick Tracy* to him in her thick accent, and he'd say, "Thanks, Mom," even if he hadn't understood a word. "She'd give me a Hershey bar every time I finished a page in my coloring book," Andy remembered.

From spending a long time at home under the care of his devoted mother, Andy grew especially close to her. He felt more distant, however, from his father, who was often away working at various jobs. "Dad was so strict," recalled his brother John, "that when you were a kid you'd think he was a mean father . . . But he made sure we had enough to eat and that it was good."

Both Andy's parents were deeply religious. Every Sunday they took him and his brothers on a three-mile walk to their Byzantine Catholic church. Inside, Andy sat through the long service and gazed up at rows of paintings of saints. In the center, above the altar, hung a copy of *The Last Supper*, a fresco by Leonardo da Vinci. Most likely this was the first fine art Andy ever saw.

On Saturday mornings when he was nine and no longer sick, Andy went to art classes, at the Carnegie Museum of Art. The Tam O'Shanter classes, named for Scottish-born Andrew Carnegie, were free, given to gifted children from all over the city. His teacher, Joseph Fitzpatrick, told the students, "Everything you look at has art." Andy and the other kids drew with ordinary crayons, then assorted media, and they studied paintings in the museum. Fitzpatrick later said, "A more talented person than Andy Warhol I never knew."

Andy continued going to Saturday art classes during his high school years. He was a bright student as well as a gifted artist. So his father saved money and set it aside to pay for two years of Andy's college education. However, his father died when Andy was thirteen and a freshman in high school.

◀ *Self-Portrait*, 1942.
Pencil on paper, 19 x 13 3/8 in.

Andy worked hard to get good grades and make his father's plans for him come true. And he kept drawing. When he was fourteen he did a remarkable self-portrait, studying his face in the mirror. Andy hated his pale skin, red pimples, and his hair, which was almost white. Boys at school teased him and called him "the albino" because he looked like someone born with the condition which results in pale skin and light hair. Ever since Andy's childhood sicknesses, the tip of his nose had become large and reddish. "Even the people in my family called me 'Andy the Red-Nosed Warhola,'" he recalled. Yet one of his classmates said, "He was oddball-looking but not oddball as a person."

At the beginning of Andy's senior year of high school, his mother became ill with colon cancer. After surgery, she re-covered but Andy and his brothers had to care for her, taking turns. His grades began to slip that year. Nevertheless, he was accepted at Carnegie Institute of Technology (Carnegie Tech).

Andy started college in September 1945, and studied painting and design. Most of the men in his classes were GIs, veterans of World War II, which ended the same year. Of course they were older than Andy. "He was like our kid . . . our little mascot," remembered Leonard Kessler, a GI and fellow student. "Andy was so shy, frightened, confused. Everybody wanted to take care of him." Kessler and a few other young men and women in Andy's classes became his friends. "All of us knew there was something so incredibly special about him," said Kessler. "We recognized that he was a genius."

Around that time Andy painted a watercolor of the living room of his family's house, where he still lived. He portrayed it in warm colors as a shabby yet comfortable place. But he never invited any of his friends over, remembered Kessler.

Andy had trouble with English, too. In a class called "Thought and Expression," some of the girls helped him write his papers. He failed anyway. Even in art classes Andy did not succeed, annoying his teachers by not following directions and doing things his own way. Students had to complete art assignments at the end of each semester that were judged by members of the faculty. Just to be different, Andy cut a painting into four parts and submitted it as four separate assignments. Some of his teachers admired his talent and originality, but others voted to drop him from the school. "Andy painted the way he wanted and they flunked him," recalled his classmate Imelda Tuttle.

When he learned about his school status, Andy went home and burst into tears. "We'll say some prayers and everything will be all right," his mother said. Sure enough, one of Andy's art teachers gave him another chance and accepted him at summer school. To help pay for the classes, Andy worked with his brother Paul. They sold fruits and vegetables from Paul's truck. While Andy was on the job he made sketches of their customers. At the end of the summer he showed his drawings to the faculty and was readmitted to Carnegie Tech. He even won a scholarship.

◀ *Living Room*, ca. 1946–1947. Watercolor and tempera on illustration board, 15 x 20 in.

▲ *Self-Portrait*, 1948. Pencil and watercolor on cardboard, 16 x 8 5/8 in.

"YOU WILL GO OFF AND YOU WILL DO SOMETHING . . . GREAT, CRAZY, TERRIFIC."

During his second year he met a new friend, Philip Pearlstein. "He [Andy] was a nice ordinary American kid," remembered Philip. With a few others they rented a barn to use as a studio. In 1948, Andy did another self-portrait in pencil and watercolor, which shows his growing skill as a draftsman. He also developed a new style of drawing with a "blotted line." He taped two sheets of paper together, then he drew in ink on one paper. Before the ink dried he pressed the drawing onto the other paper to create lively, jagged lines. In his senior year at college Andy joined the Modern Dance club. Dancing inspired him to paint a humorous Christmas card. It shows five girls posing in different dance positions. Andy entered the card in a Pittsburgh artists' exhibition. Someone wanted to buy it for seventy-five dollars, but Andy wouldn't sell because he had made the card especially for a former classmate who lived in New York.

As graduation approached, Andy wasn't sure of his future plans. "Mom, what shall I do now?" he asked Julia.

"You will go off and you will do something . . . great, crazy, terrific," she said.

Merry christmas   and   Happy New Year   from   André

Andy's friend Leonard Kessler said, "We thought he would teach, work with young children." However, Andy had become interested in fashion. He had been working part-time in a department store, painting backgrounds for window displays. With some of the money he earned he bought a white corduroy suit. He used the rest to take a trip to New York to visit museums and galleries and explore job possibilities. By the end of senior year Andy and his friend Philip both decided to become commercial artists and illustrate advertisements. "There was nothing in Pittsburgh at the time," recalled Philip. "Andy's brothers, who were his guardians, let him come to New York only on condition that he lived with me. He was still quite young. They knew my father. He also drove around Pittsburgh in his automobile, a very old Model T Ford, and sold chicken, eggs, and even fish directly to various customers. We were poor and the customers were poor." After graduation Andy and Philip packed up their things in paper shopping bags because they didn't have suitcases, and hopped on a night train bound for New York.

▲ *Christmas Card*, 1948. Tempera on folded paper, 10 3/8 x 20 1/4 in.

Andy Warhol in Manhattan, ca. 1948–1949. He carries his white corduroy jacket over his arm. ▼

"Success Is a Flying Start," ▶
from *Glamour* magazine,
September 1949

Opposite page: *Lavender Sam,* ▶
from *25 Cats Named Sam
and One Blue Pussy,* ca. 1955.
Hand-colored photo-offset print
from bound artist's book with
18 illustrations in an edition
of 190, each page 9 1/8 x 6 in.

◀ *Shoe Illustration,* from *Glamour*
magazine, September 1949

154

SUCCESS
is a
FLYING START

BY ELIZABETH WESTON

Like any good story, the Success Story has its moments of suspense. Somewhere along the way, heroine encounters problems, heroine solves problem; heroine faces danger, heroine skirts danger. It has always made interesting reading and it makes interesting living, too.

Since one in every three women in the country now works, and since each year finds more girls going into business, the chances are your personal success story will deal at least partly with a job. And you may think that isn't dangerous living. But in some ways it is.

Obviously, professional perils are not the exact counterparts of the chillers you run into in fiction. In a whole lifetime of working it's entirely possible that you'll never once totter on the brink of a precipice or be held captive by foreign spies. Nor will you find that all the dangers come at the end of the story—quite the contrary; they begin at exactly nine o'clock on the first Monday morning. And the girl who learns to recognize and side-step them early is truly off to a flying start. So watch out for:

The danger of dubious decorum, and of course we don't mean the gum-chewing, slang-talking kind of error. What we mean is this: success doesn't come in one fell swoop—it sneaks up on you. One week you're a junior messenger and the next you're a secretary. Of course, it means a new desk and new duties. With a bit more salary and a bit more contact, you'll probably make a few improvements in your wardrobe. But what

about your attitude? Take talk. What you had to say about anything relating to business when you were a junior messenger was taken as pure personal opinion. But it's different now. What you say is apt to be noised around as what your boss said ... which means that you have to weigh your words a bit more carefully. There's the beginning of limelight on you, and as you very well know, limelight accentuates everything—faults as well as virtues. Which leads us on to pitfall number two:

The danger of inflated ego. If you have any tendency to swank (and most of us like to show off a little), success gives you a dangerous opportunity to indulge it. A look-at-me-I'm-office-manager attitude is just about the best way we know to become an ex-office manager. At the very least, it will antagonize all the people without whose cooperation you can't get along. But such an attitude can be and should be stifled far below the office manager level. You can begin the very first time you're singled out for any professional distinction. The day the boss says to you, "Your filing system is more efficient than Mary's," would you mind showing her how it works?," watch out. Remind yourself that you've been there six weeks longer than Mary. Remind yourself that she does half again as many letters as you. Remind yourself of anything and everything that will keep a note of superiority out of your voice. Then mention pleasantly, "Mr. X suggested that it might save time if we coordinated our filing systems. Do you think you'll have (Continued on page 172)

He had made the shoes look as though they had been worn. Tina wanted them to look brand new. So Andy went back to the apartment and re-did the drawings. This time they were perfect. The illustrations were published in the magazine in September 1949. Accidentally, the "a" of Andy's last name was dropped. His credit read "Andy Warhol," and from then on, that's what he called himself.

"Andy was a special talent," recalled Philip, "an amazing talent. He was very quiet, very modest. He would sit up all night working on jobs he got. He always had jobs to do."

At the end of the summer they had to find another place to live, so they sublet space in a dance studio.

Then Andy changed his look. Instead of getting dressed up for interviews, he wore chinos (khakis), T-shirts, and old sneakers. He carried his artwork in a brown paper bag. So his friends nicknamed him "Raggedy Andy" and "Andy Paperbag."

One assignment led to another. He hired Nathan Gluck to assist him. "I helped him with the preliminary drawings of shoes, jewelry, and greeting cards," said Nathan. "I would draw them and Andy would correct them . . . I did the mechanical work [pasting on type] so that he could go out and get more jobs. He was so eager to make money."

Andy earned enough to rent his own apartment. When his mother, Julia, visited him, she thought it was "a terrible place," dirty and full of mice. Andy's brothers had already

They sublet a cheap apartment only for the summer and began looking for work. "We were desperate for money," remembered Philip. He and Andy carried samples of their art in portfolios. Andy dressed up in his "white corduroy suit that gradually went yellow," said Philip. "It was a very heavy corduroy and it was a very hot summer. It was unpleasant to wear the suit but Andy wore it anyway, with a necktie." On his second day in New York, Andy went to see Tina Fredericks, the art director of the prestigious *Glamour* magazine. Despite, or perhaps because of, his odd appearance, she liked him and liked his artwork. "I need some drawings of shoes, Mr. Warhola," said Tina. "I need them tomorrow morning at ten o'clock. Can you do them?"

The next morning he showed up at ten with the drawings.

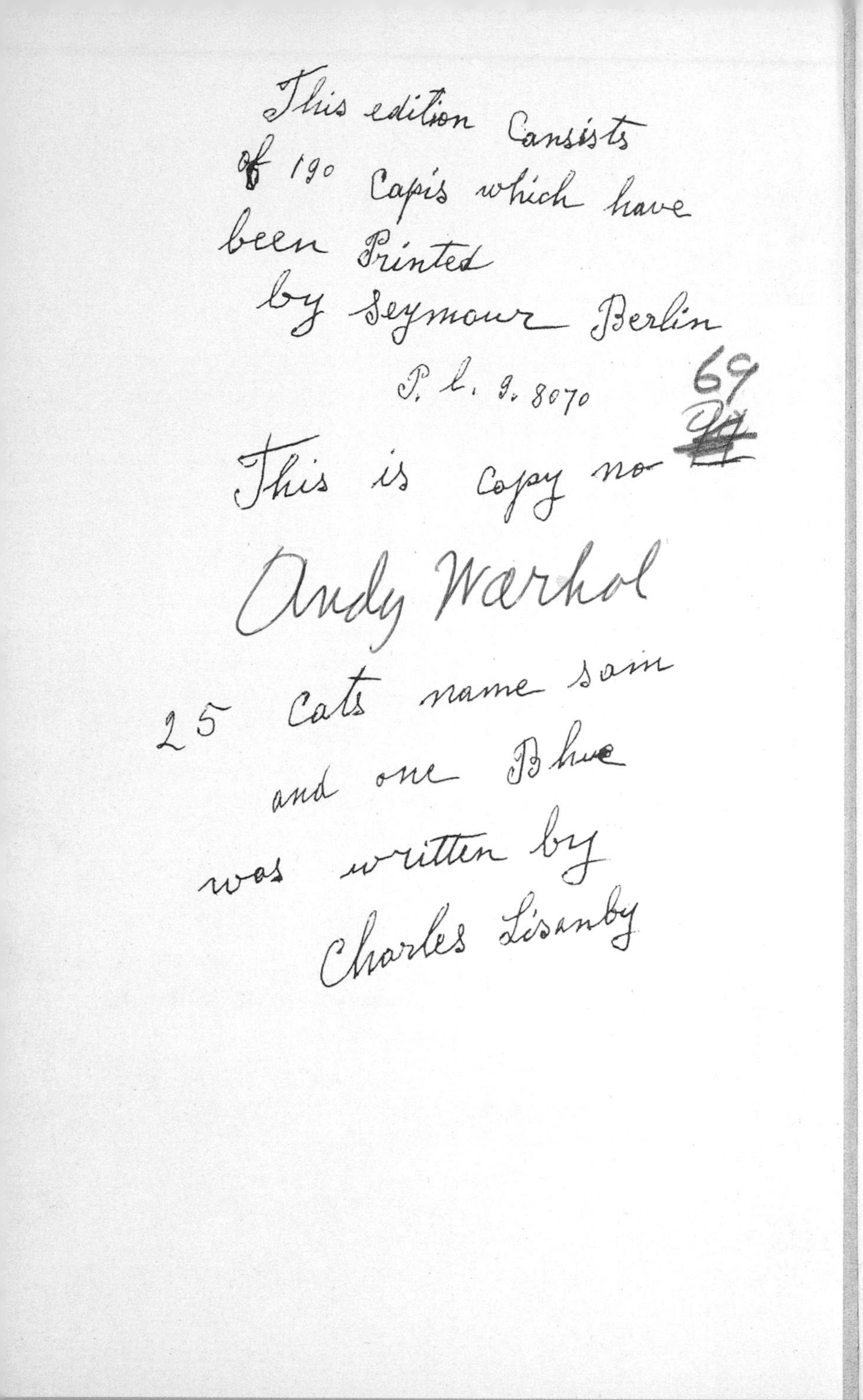

This edition Consists
of 190 Copis which have
been Printed
by Seymour Berlin
P. L. 9. 8070   69
94
This is   copy no.

Andy Warhol

25 Cats name sam
and one Blue
was   written by
Charles Lisanby

Sam

moved out of her house and she now lived alone. She decided to go to New York to take care of Andy and keep his place clean. And to make sure he ate something besides cake and candy.

To catch the mice Andy adopted a Siamese cat named Hester. Soon he adopted another Siamese, and his mother named this one Sam. Before long Hester and Sam had kittens—all called Sam. Andy did a book of drawings about them. Each page features a different Sam colored in lavender or pink, with Hester, smiling, in blue. Andy liked his mother's old-fashioned penmanship, so he asked her to write the names of the cats in script on the pages.

Butterflies, 1955. ▶
Hand-colored photo-offset
print, 13 3/4 x 10 in.

Andy had a limited edition of the book printed and then colored each by hand at home with friends. He assigned the colors. "Somebody would do red, then blue," said Nathan. "Andy never wanted an even flat color. Some places were lighter and [other areas were] darker." Andy gave the books to his friends. But in hopes of getting commissioned work for magazines, Andy also gave copies of the cat book to art directors.

He also presented them with traditional Easter eggs he and his mother had decorated. "The Rusyn Pysanky eggs are done with a head of a pin on an end of a stick or pencil," recalled Andy's nephew James. "When it's dipped in hot wax and stroked onto an egg it creates a mark that is a big dot with a tail." Usually the eggs were dyed, then the wax was removed, leaving the marks as white. Andy's mother "parted a little from this tradition by adding crayons to the wax to darken the marks," said James. "And then the eggs wouldn't get dyed but just be kept plain . . . Julia [Andy's mother] was a master at this and she passed it on to Andy and to many of her grandchildren."

For another gift to send art directors, Andy hand-colored wrapping paper that he printed with typical Carpatho-Rusyn Easter decorations—birds, butterflies, suns, stars, and flowers. In 1955 these presents landed him an important assignment: a women's shoe company named I. Miller hired Andy to illustrate its weekly ads for *The New York Times* newspaper. Andy's unusual black-and-white drawings won awards. He was called "the Leonardo da Vinci of the shoe trade."

More and more jobs poured in. Around this time he and Julia moved into a larger apartment they shared with Andy's old friend Leonard Kessler. Kessler had become a children's book writer and illustrator. Sometimes Andy asked him to help finish a project to get it done on time. "I helped him with a lot of those shoes," remembered Kessler. "Andy and I would sketch them up. He rarely had to do a thing over again. He got it right the first time. His drawing was magnificent."

"I have some early memories of him working very diligently at his drawing table with a pile of shoes next to his desk," recalled his nephew James, who sometimes came to visit. "To watch him draw was quite mesmerizing. His drawing ability was incredible. He drew with a confident sure-handedness that was not only exact but full of expression."

"TO WATCH HIM DRAW WAS QUITE MESMERIZING. HIS DRAWING ABILITY WAS INCREDIBLE. HE DREW WITH A CONFIDENT SURE-HANDEDNESS THAT WAS NOT ONLY EXACT BUT FULL OF EXPRESSION."

The autobiography of alice B. shoe.

Any one for shoes ?

Sunset and evening shoe

Dial M for shoe.

Shoe of the evening, beautiful shoe.

A composite of Andy Warhol's hand-colored offset prints for *A la Recherche du Shoe Perdu*, 1955. In the original portfolio, each illustration is centered on its own page.

Andy Warhol at Home with his Mother, 1966 ▶

For another advertising piece for I. Miller, Andy illustrated a gorgeous portfolio of "shoe poems" written by his pal Ralph Pomeroy. Each page featured a large drawing of a fancy high-heeled shoe with a silly one-line "poem": "Shoe of the evening, beautiful shoe," and "Anyone for shoes?"

To finish art for the book, Andy gathered his friends together at his favorite ice-cream parlor, Serendipity 3, for a "coloring party." Over hot-fudge sundaes, "frozen hot chocolate," and banana splits, everyone pitched in and colored the printed drawings with Dr. Martin's dyes, a kind of ink. Andy did some of the pages himself in watercolor. For the final touch he asked his mom to write out the poems by hand in her old-fashioned script. The owners of Serendipity 3 admired Andy's work. They kept some of the drawings, hung them on the walls, and sold them.

Andy's shoe drawings attracted attention, but so did he. Andy wanted to appear shabby, as though he were so rich that he didn't care how he looked! He went around town with his shoelaces deliberately untied. If he had a new pair of shoes he'd spill paint on them or soak them in water to make them look old. And he could never tie his tie properly. One end was always longer than the other. "When he couldn't make the ends match up, he just cut them off," recalled his assistant, Nathan. It drove Andy's mother crazy. As Andy's hair thinned on top and he started to get bald, he wore a wig. First brown, then different shades of gray, silver, and white. He didn't put the wigs on straight and he never combed them. "He slapped them on," said Nathan. "You couldn't miss him, a skinny creep with his silver wig," recalled Frederick Eberstadt, a rich socialite. "Andy wanted so much to be beautiful," said his friend Charles Lisanby, "but he wore that terrible wig which didn't fit and only looked awful."

Andy used his wig and strange appearance to show that he was unique. As soon as art directors looked at his work, they saw that it was special as well and hired him. Andy earned a great deal of money as a commercial illustrator. In 1960 he bought a four-story town house on Lexington Avenue in New York City for his mother and himself. He filled the rooms with flea market finds—a life-sized Mr. Peanut, antique toys, merry-go-round figures, penny-arcade machines, and cookie jars. Once he stopped at F.A.O. Schwartz, a huge toy store, and bought a teddy bear. He strolled down Fifth Avenue with the bear, unwrapped, tucked under his arm. People must have stared. "I knew I was putting on airs by carrying the bear," said Andy, "but I just felt like it."

At home his mother took charge of the kitchen, the cats, and a talking parrot. "The cats were very mysterious," remembered Andy's nephew James, who often stayed at the house. "Usually they only came out at night when Bubba [a Carpathian-Rusyn word meaning grandmother] would feed them behind the Dutch doors in the kitchen. They would glide down the stairs very quietly one by one when everyone was asleep and on occasion if you were lucky you'd see one."

Every morning Andy's mother fixed breakfast for him and they said a prayer together. "My Andy can do no wrong," she said. "He's a good boy."

Andy began to collect fine art. He enjoyed his work as a commercial artist, but he wanted to become a painter and be recognized as a serious artist. "I want to be as famous as the Queen of England," he once said. In those days the most acclaimed artists were Abstract Expressionists based in New York. Critics throughout the world regarded them as "modern masters." With loose brushstrokes and drips of paint, artists such as Jackson Pollock and Willem de Kooning created enormous, powerful pictures to express their feelings and ideas. Andy's work did not resemble theirs at all.

In contrast, and as a reaction to the Abstract Expressionists, a group of younger artists created work with a greater sense of fun. They found old bottles, newspapers, and torn clothes in the city streets and attached the junk to their paintings. They painted pictures of ordinary, everyday things: light bulbs, coffee cans, magazine ads, and comic strips.

Andy saw this new work at galleries and at the Museum of Modern Art's exhibit "Sixteen Americans" in 1959. He decided to make gigantic paintings of *his* favorite cartoon characters: Dick Tracy, Superman, and Popeye. "They were things I knew," he said. Andy fastened a piece of canvas to the wall and projected a comic book image onto it. Then he traced the parts he wanted to keep. He painted original colors and left patches bare. One day at a gallery, Andy saw the cartoon paintings of artist Roy Lichtenstein. He realized they were both doing the same kind of thing at the same time. But Lichtenstein's paintings were better.

Andy felt discouraged. "I've got to think of something different," he said.

The story goes that one evening in 1960, when Andy was thirty-two, his friend Muriel Latow came over to visit. She owned an art gallery and Andy asked her for advice. Muriel said, "You should paint something that everybody sees every day . . . like a can of soup."

For the first time that evening, Andy smiled.

100 Cans, 1962. ▶

Oil on canvas, 72 x 52 in.

The next morning Andy sent his mother out to buy one of each of the thirty-two varieties of Campbell's soup. First he sketched them. Then he hit on the idea of making "portraits—" as his friend, art critic David Bourdon, was to call them—of each can of soup set against a plain white background. An art dealer from Los Angeles, California, came to Andy's studio. He offered to show the pictures that summer.

Andy's "Soup Can" paintings stirred up excitement. Portraits traditionally represented important people like kings or wealthy citizens and their families. No other artist had ever made portraits of soup cans before. "Tomato soup will never be just tomato soup again," said a critic. Some people laughed at Andy. A supermarket stacked Campbell's soup in the window with a sign that read, "the real thing for only 29 cents a can." Andy used the put-down for publicity. He took a photographer to the market and had his picture taken signing the cans of soup. The photo appeared in newspapers everywhere. Many people were puzzled, though. How could Andy call these paintings "art" when he had simply copied the familiar red-and-white labels? Did he really think ordinary food cans were good subjects?

Andy said, "I just paint things I always thought were beautiful . . . things you use every day and never think about."

Why Campbell's soups? asked interviewers.

"They're things I had when I was a child," said Andy.

Over the next two years he continued to paint a series of Campbell's soup cans. Sometimes he used stencils to make the cans exactly alike except for the flavors. Other times he painted enormous individual still lifes. Or sad-looking soup cans with torn labels. He used a variety of media: pencil, ink, crayons, acrylic and oil paints. "He didn't have any easels," recalled his nephew James, who visited during this period. "He either worked at his drafting table with smaller pieces or on the floor or against a wall if they were larger. There were numerous paintings in rolls and on stretchers that were everywhere. The linen canvas created a pleasant unique smell that permeated most of the upper floors."

For his next subject Andy chose the Coca-Cola bottle. A black-and-white painting almost six feet high shows a giant-sized bottle. Another painting in green depicts 210 Coca-Cola bottles. "What does Coca-Cola mean to you?" asked an interviewer.

"Pop," joked Andy, using another word for soda. He was also referring to the new movement in painting that was named "Pop Art."

Then he asked his friend Muriel what else he could paint. "You should paint pictures of money," she said.

"Oh, gee," said Andy. "That really is a great idea!"

In pencil he drew larger-than-life pictures of one-dollar bills and ten-dollar bills. Then Andy thought of showing rows and rows and rows of bills. To do this he developed a technique using silkscreens. First he did a drawing. He took the drawing to a printing shop, where it was made into a stencil on a fabric screen. Back in his studio Andy placed a large canvas on the floor and stretched the silkscreen over it. He poured paint into a corner of the framed screen and pushed the paint across the surface with a squeegee. Paint went through the porous silk. Over and over Andy repeated the same image. "The reason I paint this way is that I want to be a machine," he said. When an assistant helped him, the work went faster.

Andy's style of producing art with a team of assistants became his trademark. With helpers he was able to turn out more art at a faster pace. Working in this manner was not new to the art world. Artists such as Leonardo da Vinci and Sandro Botticelli in the fifteenth century had started their careers as teenage apprentices in the workshops of master painters. They had helped their masters complete commissioned works just as Andy's assistants helped him. People enjoyed working for Andy, even without pay, because he made projects so much fun. Andy kept searching for unusual subjects and unusual ways to paint them.

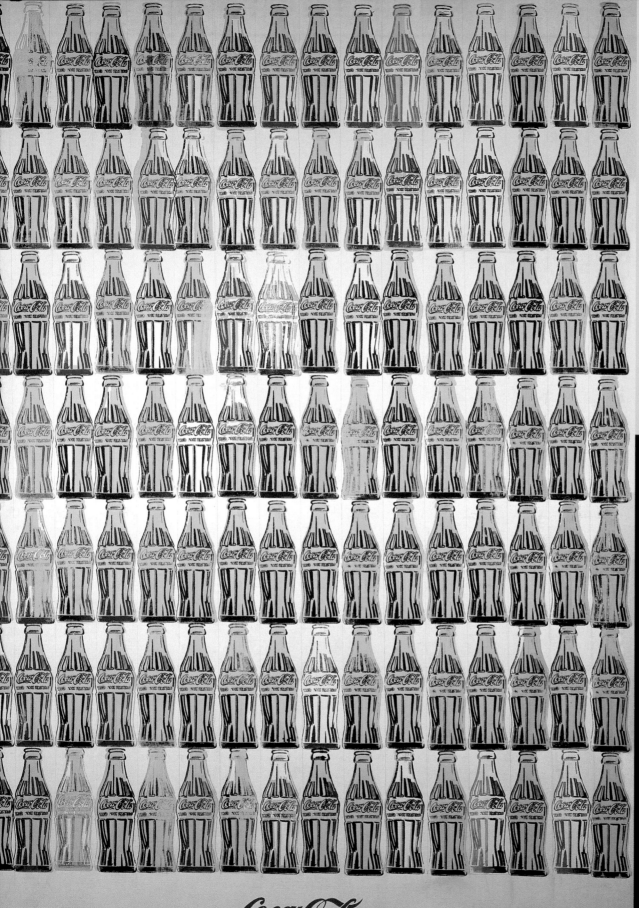

Green Coca-Cola Bottles, 1962.
Acrylic on canvas, 82 1/4 x 57 in.

He got his next idea from his nephew James. Once, when James was seven, he and his family drove in from Pittsburgh for a visit. Andy gave James five dollars to buy something for himself at the variety store across the street. James usually chose car models with his spending money, but this time he bought a "Do It Yourself" art kit. The kit contained tubes of paint, brushes, and an ordinary sailboat picture. The picture was divided into numbered sections. The numbers matched paint colors so that people could choose the "right" ones. "Andy decided to use it [the sailboat picture] as one of his paintings," recalled James. Andy was poking fun at this art, which did not encourage originality.

"He would use an opaque projector to enlarge and transfer his images," said James. The projector sat on a table. Andy put the sailboat picture underneath the top lid, then projected the image onto the wall, adjusting the size with the lens. The projector magnified the picture so that Andy could trace it onto a large canvas, six feet high by almost nine feet wide. Then he painted in his *own* colors. Lavender, peach, and purple for the sailboat painting. "He had a wonderful sense of color, putting strange colors together," recalled Leonard Kessler. Andy purposely left some sections blank, while dotting other spaces with press-on numbers. "He allowed me to rub on many of the numbers," said James. "He didn't dictate too much of where he wanted them. He just showed me how to do it and then let it be up to me."

Do It Yourself (Sailboats), 1962. Acrylic and Prestype on canvas, 72 x 100 in. ▶

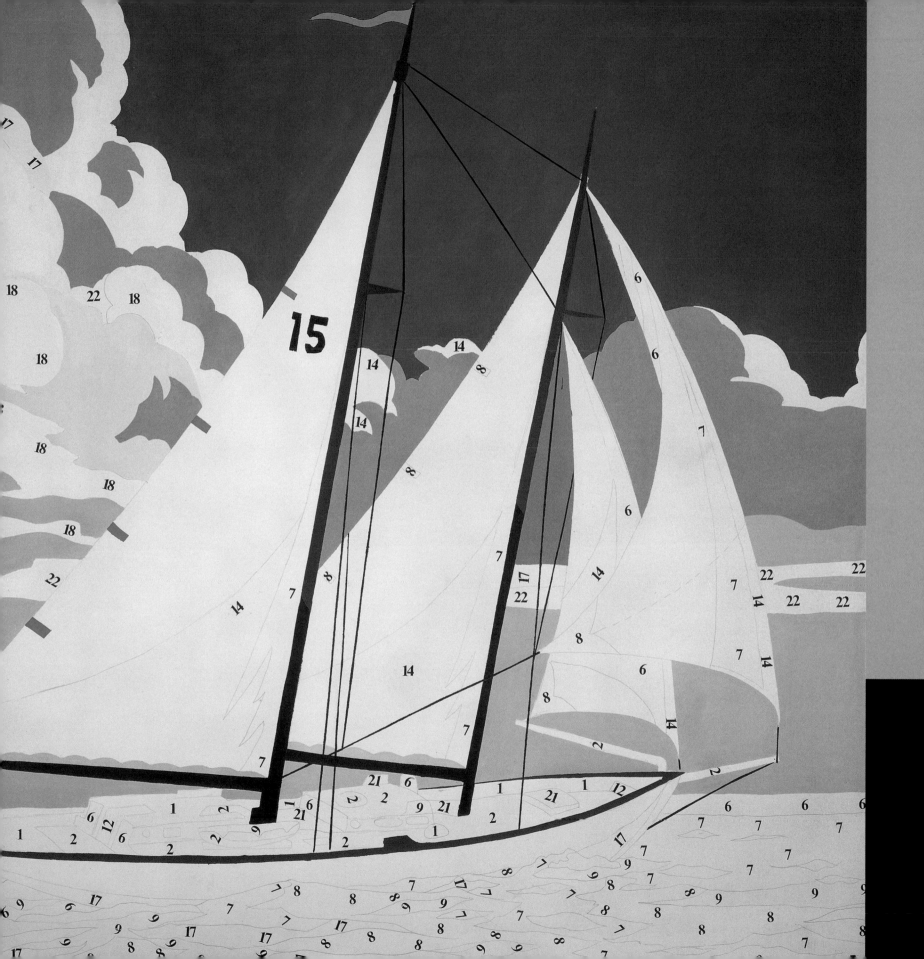

Marilyn Monroe, 1962.
Acrylic on canvas,
20 x 16 in.

ANDY'S LOVE OF MOVIES GREATLY INFLUENCED THE NEXT PHASE OF HIS PAINTING. IT ALL BEGAN WITH MARILYN MONROE.

Andy's love of movies greatly influenced the next phase of his painting. It all began with Marilyn Monroe. During the summer of 1962, Andy's soup can pictures were shown at the Ferus Gallery in Los Angeles, California. The day after the show closed, movie star Marilyn Monroe died. She was only thirty-six years old. Andy, a lifelong movie fan, had adored Monroe and had even met her in person. "She fascinated me as she did the rest of America," he said. He felt inspired to do a series of "printed paintings" about her.

Andy bought a black-and-white photograph of Marilyn and had it made into a silkscreen. He screened a single image of her face onto small canvases. Then he multiplied her image in *Six Marilyns*, *Marilyn Twenty Times*, and *One Hundred Marilyns*. In some of the pictures he hand-painted the shapes of her hair, eyes, and lips first. Then he printed over the shapes of her features with the silkscreen. For *Gold Marilyn Monroe* he painted an entire canvas with gold paint. In the center he added a single image of her face with the silkscreen.

Eleanor Ward, owner of the Stable Gallery in New York, admired Andy's work and offered to give him a one-man show in November 1962. On opening night people crowded the gallery. Andy's mother handed out soup can buttons. When Andy arrived he discovered that architect Philip Johnson, founder and director of the Architecture and Design Department at the Museum of Modern Art in New York, had already bought *Gold Marilyn Monroe*. Johnson then gave the painting to the museum for its permanent collection. Andy was becoming famous!

In December a public conference was held at the Museum of Modern Art. A panel of critics, curators, and art historians discussed the new art movement. Many people in the audience hated it and hissed and booed. But panelists defended the art. They named it "Pop Art," short for "popular" culture. Andy was considered one of the leading artists, a spokesman. He had blurred the line between commercial art—illustrations used primarily for advertising—and fine art, which was seen as work highly worthy in and of itself (not for its monetary value). "Pop Art is for everyone," he said. Some critics said that his pictures of dollars, Coca-Cola bottles, and movie stars represented America. Andy said, "I just paint those objects in my paintings because those are the things I know best . . . I think of myself as an American artist."

ANDY HAD THE BRICK WALLS PAINTED SILVER AND THE CONCRETE WALLS COVERED WITH TIN FOIL.

With the growing demand for his work, Andy needed a bigger studio. In 1964 he found an empty loft in a warehouse building on East Forty-seventh Street in New York. His friends called it "the Factory." Andy had the brick walls painted silver and the concrete walls covered with tin foil. Even the floors were painted silver. Andy wore a silver wig to match. Now he sported a black leather jacket, tight black jeans, and dark glasses.

"Children were drawn to Andy like a comic character with his wig askew, glasses and . . . jeans," remembered Bob Colacello, who worked for him for twelve years. "Andy loved to talk to kids. He found it interesting."

People of all ages loved coming to the Factory. "It was a constant open house," said Andy, "like a children's TV program—you just hung around and characters you knew dropped in."

▲ *Andy Warhol in the Factory*, 1967

◄ **Opposite page:** *Andy Warhol in the Factory*, 1967

Despite his many visitors, Andy found time to create new work. His next big show was at the Leo Castelli Gallery in New York, which specialized in Pop Art. Andy filled the rooms with silkscreened paintings of flowers in brilliant Day-Glo colors. For his second show Andy decorated the gallery from floor to ceiling with *Cow Wallpaper*. He repeated a huge silkscreened image of a cow's head in bright pink on a bright yellow background.

Andy's fame spread throughout the world. Over the next two decades he had many exhibitions. In Paris, France, he exhibited his flower paintings. In Zurich, Switzerland, he showed pictures based on his toy collection: a ship, a police car, an emergency helicopter, a robot, a panda beating a drum, and a clown riding a scooter. He hung the pictures low so that

children could easily see them. "Kids seem to like my work," said Andy.

Adults did, too. Famous people hired him to paint their portraits. Or Andy chose subjects just *because* they were famous, such as Chairman Mao of China, boxer Muhammad Ali, and, of course, himself. In 1983 he even did portraits of animals on the list of endangered species: the Bald Eagle, the African elephant, and the Black Rhino (which he painted blue).

Andy Warhol passed away in 1987, but his work today is celebrated worldwide and is shown continually in museums. A reporter once asked him, "Did you ever imagine when you painted your first soup can, that it would become art?"

"No," said Andy. "It's like anything. You just work. If it happens, it happens."

TIME LINE

1928

◀ *Andy Warhol, 1986*

1937–1941

1942

1934-1936

1936-1937

1945

1949

1950–1952

Andy has many assignments as a commercial illustrator, drawing pictures for advertisements in magazines.

1952

Andy's mother comes to New York and moves into his apartment on East Seventy-fifth Street. They have two Siamese cats, which quickly multiply.

1960

Andy buys a town house on Lexington Avenue for his mother and himself. He starts collecting folk art and fine art and wants to become a serious painter. He paints a series of pictures of Campbell's soup cans.

1962

Andy paints and draws images from "Do It Yourself" kits. He develops a technique that combines silkscreens with painting and does a series of repeated images featuring Coca-Cola bottles and dollar bills. He has a one-man show at the Ferus Gallery in Los Angeles, California, and creates a series of "printed paintings" in homage to actress Marilyn Monroe. In November he has a one-man show at the Stable Gallery in New York. Architect Philip Johnson, director of the Architecture and

1953-1955

Andy makes gifts for various art directors. He becomes the most sought after illustrator of women's accessories and earns a very good living.

1955

Andy self-publishes his book of cat drawings.

I. Miller, a women's shoe company, hires him to illustrate their weekly ads for *The New York Times* newspaper.

▼ *Emergency (Helicopter)*, 1983. Acrylic and silkscreen on canvas, 11 x 14 1/8 in.

1962

Design Department at the Museum of Modern Art in New York, buys *Gold Marilyn Monroe* and presents it to the museum. This purchase gives Andy's work great credence in the art world. The Nelson Art Gallery (now the Nelson-Atkins Museum of Art) in Kansas City, Missouri, buys Andy's baseball painting for their collection. A panel of experts at the Museum of Modern Art chooses the name "Pop Art" for the new movement of which Andy is considered one of the leading artists.

1963

Andy rents a firehouse for his studio.

1964

Andy moves his studio to a loft in a warehouse on East Forty-seventh Street and calls it the Factory. He starts making offbeat underground movies starring his men and women friends.

In April he has a show of his grocery carton and Brillo box sculptures at the Stable Gallery. In November he switches dealers and shows his "Flowers" at the Leo Castelli Gallery in New York. He does a series of portraits of Jacqueline Kennedy.

1967

Andy lectures at colleges and moves his Factory to Union Square in New York City. He does a series of self-portraits in acrylic and silkscreen.

1968

Andy has another solo museum exhibit, this time at the Modern Museum in Stockholm. The show then travels through Scandinavia. In June actress Valerie Solanas, a radical feminist, comes to the Factory and shoots Andy in the stomach and lungs. Later Valerie claims that Andy promised to produce her screenplay but didn't do it.

1965

Andy goes to Paris, France, for the opening of his "Flowers" exhibit at the Sonnabend Gallery. He has his first solo museum exhibit at the Institute of Contemporary Art at the University of Pennsylvania.

1966

Andy concentrates on filmmaking. Leo Castelli exhibits Andy's *Cow Wallpaper* and the *Silver Clouds*.

1968

Andy is rushed to the hospital and pronounced dead. However, doctors massage his heart and revive him. He undergoes surgery and spends two months in the hospital.

1969

Andy starts publishing a magazine, *Interview: A Monthly Film Journal*.

1970

Andy has another one-man show, a retrospective at the Pasadena Art Museum (now the Norton Simon Museum of Art) in Pasadena, California. Andy's mother's health declines and she becomes senile. She suffers a stroke and returns to Pittsburgh where John and Paul take care of her. After suffering a second stroke she moves into a nursing home. Andy calls her frequently but never sees her again.

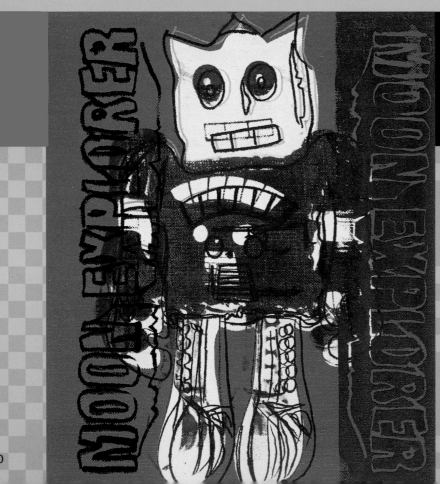

◄ *Moon Explorer Robot*, 1983.
Synthetic polymer paint and
silkscreen on canvas, 14 x 11 in.

1973

Andy makes pencil drawings and a series of silkscreened paintings of Chairman Mao of China.

1971

Andy exhibits his *Cow Wallpaper* at the Whitney Museum of American Art in New York.

1972

Andy focuses on painting again and does a series of portraits of celebrities, movie stars, and political figures. His mother dies in Pittsburgh. He feels a deep loss and paints several portraits of her.

1974

Andy moves his private residence to East Sixty-sixth Street, and he moves the Factory to Broadway. He continues his series of portraits. A major retrospective of his work is shown at the Kunsthaus in Zurich, Switzerland.

1979–1980

The Whitney Museum of American Art exhibits Andy's portraits.
Andy produces a portfolio, *Ten Portraits of Jews of the Twentieth Century*.

1983-1985

Andy makes the *Endangered Species* series. In December he attends the opening of his exhibition "Pictures for Children" at the Bruno Bischofberger Gallery in Zurich, Switzerland.

The Campbell Soup Company hires Andy to create a new series of paintings of their dry soup mixes.

▲ *Andy Warhol with Children at the Opening of "Pictures for Children," 1983*

1986

Andy begins a series of silkscreened paintings using the camouflage pattern. He is commissioned to create a series of artworks based on Leonardo da Vinci's *The Last Supper*.

1987

Andy flies to Milan, Italy, for the opening of his *Last Supper* exhibition.

Back in New York he has a routine gallbladder operation. He takes a turn for the worse and dies of complications the next day, February 22, 1987, at the age of fifty-eight.

GLOSSARY

Art dealer: someone who displays and represents an artist's work

Art movement: a new way of painting, sculpting, or photographing that is shared by like-minded artists and is given a name by critics or art historians

Canvas: fabric on which an artist paints

Commercial artists: people who are hired to create pictures that are used for advertising in newspapers and magazines

Fine artists: people who create works of art—fine art—that meet their own standards of beauty without regard to sales and public opinion

Draftsman: an artist who is exceptionally skilled in drawing

Fashion: clothing and other articles that are popular in a certain period of time

Illustration: a picture that explains, clarifies, or decorates words

Leonardo da Vinci: (1452–1519) a fifteenth-century artist, scientist, and inventor who painted masterpieces such as *The Last Supper* and *Mona Lisa*

Limited edition: a certain small number of copies made of a book or set of drawings

Medium: the materials an artist uses to make pictures, including pencil, ink, pastels, crayons, and paint

One-man show: an exhibit devoted exclusively to the work of a single artist

Pop Art: the school of art that features images taken from popular culture

Portfolios: flat cases for carrying samples of an artist's work

Portraits: paintings and drawings of people or animals (or soup cans!) that capture a physical likeness or reveal character and inner spirit

Self-portrait: a picture that an artist paints, draws, or photographs of himself or herself.

Silkscreens: mesh stencils used for color printing

Sketched: drawn quickly, loosely, without details

Stencils: patterns that have been cut out or rubbed onto one surface, then used to apply the image to another surface

Still lifes: pictures of inanimate or non-living objects

Studio: the workroom of an artist

Watercolor: blocks or tubes of paint that are mixed with water

SOURCE NOTES

Page 4. "I drew pictures . . . We made pictures together." Julia Warhola quoted in Victor Bockris, *The Life and Death of Andy Warhol* (New York: Bantam Books, 1989), p.15.

Page 4. "He just loved . . . crayons." John Warhola, ibid., p.17.

Page 4. "I used to have . . . soup and a sandwich." Andy Warhol quoted in Kenneth Goldsmith (ed.), *I'll Be Your Mirror: The Selected Andy Warhol Interviews* (New York: Carroll & Graf Publishers, 2004), p.18.

Page 4. "Many an afternoon . . . to this day." Andy Warhol quoted in Bockris, p.105.

Page 5. "They all sang . . . Rusyn craft traditions." James Warhola quoted in an e-mail letter to the author, May 19, 2005.

Page 5. "Flowers sculptures . . . The tin flowers . . . good and correct artist." Andy Warhol quoted in ibid., p. 12.

Page 5. "He was a good little artist . . . second grade." The Andy Warhol Museum quoted in Jan Greenberg and Sandra Jordan, *Andy Warhol: Prince of Pop* (New York: Delacorte Books for Young Readers, 2004), p. 6.

Page 5. "I never wanted . . . a tap dancer." Andy Warhol quoted in Goldsmith, p. 89.

Page 7. "Thanks, Mom . . . coloring book." Andy Warhol quoted in *The Philosophy of Andy Warhol (From A to B and Back Again)* (New York: a Harvest Book, Harcourt, Inc., 1975), p. 22.

Page 7. "Dad was so strict . . . that it was good." John Warhola quoted in Bockris, pp. 12–13.

Page 7. "Everything you look at . . . I never knew." Joseph Fitzpatrick quoted in ibid., p. 29.

Page 9. "the albino." A Schenley High School graduate quoted in ibid., p. 31.

Page 9. "Even the people . . . Red-Nosed Warhola." Andy Warhol quoted in *The Philosophy of Andy Warhol*, p. 63.

Page 9. "He was oddball-looking . . . as a person." A Schenley High School graduated quoted in Bockris, p. 31.

Page 9. "He was like . . . was a genius." Leonard Kessler quoted in an interview with the author, August 25, 2004.

Page 11. "Andy painted . . . they flunked him." Imelda Tuttle quoted in David Bourdon, *Warhol* (New York: Harry N. Abrams, Inc., 1995), p. 21.

Page 11. "We'll say . . . be all right." John Warhola quoted in Bockris, p, 37.

Page 12. "He [Andy] was . . . American kid." Philip Pearlstein quoted in an interview with the author, May 10, 2005.

Page 12. "blotted line." Bourdon quoted in *Warhol*, p. 29.

Page 12. "Mom, what . . . crazy, terrific." Julia Warhola quoted in ibid., p.22.

Page 13. "We thought . . . young children." Leonard Kessler quoted in an interview with the author, August 25, 2004.

Page 13. "There was nothing . . . customers were poor." Philip Pearlstein quoted in an interview with the author, May 10, 2005.

Page 14. "We were desperate for money." Ibid.

Page 14. "white corduroy . . . with a necktie." Ibid.

Page 14. "I need some . . . you do them?" Tina Fredricks quoted in Bockris, p. 51.

Page 14. "Andy was a . . . jobs to do." Philip Pearlstein quoted in an interview with the author, May 10, 2005.

Page 14. "Raggedy Andy." Andy's friends quoted in ibid., p. 52.

Page 14. "Andy Paperbag." Andy Warhol quoted in Wayne Koestenbaum, *Andy Warhol* (New York: A Lipper/Viking Book, 2001), p. 1.

Page 14. "I helped him . . . to make money." Nathan Gluck quoted in an interview with the author, May 12, 2005.

Page 14. "a terrible place." Julia Warhola quoted in Bockris, p.66.

Page 17. "Somebody would do . . . and [other areas were] darker." Nathan Gluck quoted in an interview with the author, May 12, 2005.

Page 17. "The Rusyn Pysanky eggs . . . her grandchildren." James Warhola quoted in an e-mail letter to the author, May 19, 2005.

Page 17. "the Leonardo . . . shoe trade." *Women's Wear Daily* quoted in Bourdon, Warhol, p. 42.

Page 17. "I helped . . . drawing was magnificent." Leonard Kessler quoted in an interview with the author, August 25, 2004.

Page 17. "I have some early . . . full of expression." James Warhola quoted in an e-mail letter to the author, May 22, 2005.

Page 19. "shoe poems." Ralph Pomeroy quoted in Bourdon, p. 43.

Page 19. "Shoe of . . . for shoes?" Ibid., p. 45.

Page 19. "coloring party." Ibid., p. 44.

Page 19. "When he couldn't . . . cut them off." A visitor to Andy's Lexington Avenue apartment quoted in Bockris, p. 72.

Page 19. "He slapped them on." Nathan Gluck quoted in an interview with the author, May 12, 2005.

Page 19. "You couldn't miss . . . silver wig." Frederick Eberstadt quoted in Bockris, ibid., p. 102.

Page 19. "Andy wanted . . . only looked awful." Charles Lisanby quoted in ibid., p. 81.

Page 19. "I knew I was . . . felt like it." Andy Warhol quoted in Bob Colacello, *Holy Terror: Andy Warhol Close Up* (New York: HarperCollins, 1990), p. 174.

Page 19. "The cats were . . . lucky you'd see one." James Warhola quoted in an e-mail letter to the author, May 19, 2005.

Page 19. "My Andy . . . a good boy." Julia Warhola quoted in Bockris, p.91.

Page 20. "I want to be . . . Queen of England." Andy Warhol quoted in ibid., p. 102.

Page 20. "modern masters." Bourdon, p. 62.

Page 20. "They were things I knew." Andy Warhol quoted in Goldsmith, p. 99.

Page 20. "I've got to think of something different." Andy Warhol quoted in Bockris, p. 97.

Page 20. "You should . . . can of soup." Muriel Latow quoted by Ted Carey in ibid., p. 105.

Page 23. "portraits." David Bourdon quoted in Bourdon, p. 109.

Page 23. "Tomato soup . . . soup again." Ivan Karp quoted in Bourdon, p. 90.

Page 23. "the real thing . . . a can." Colacello, p. 27.

Page 23. "I just paint . . . never think about." Andy Warhol quoted in *Time*, May 11,1962, quoted in Bockris, p. 110.

Page 23. "They're things . . . was a child." Andy Warhol quoted in Goldsmith, p. 5.

Page 23. "He didn't have . . . the upper floors." James Warhola quoted in an e-mail letter to the author, May 19, 2005.

Page 24. "What does . . . Pop." Andy Warhol and KG, an interviewer for *Art Voices*, December 1962, quoted in ibid., p. 5.

Page 24. "You should . . . a great idea!" Muriel Latow and Andy Warhol quoted by Ted Carey in Bockris, p. 105.

Page 24. "The reason . . . be a machine." Andy Warhol quoted by G.R. Swenson in an interview for *Art News* quoted in Bourdon, p. 140.

Page 26. "Andy decided to use . . . transfer his images." James Warhola quoted in an e-mail letter to the author, May 19, 2005.

Page 26. "He had a . . . strange colors together." Leonard Kessler quoted in interview with the author, August 25, 2004.

Page 26. "He allowed me . . . up to me." James Warhola quoted in an e-mail letter to the author, May 19, 2005.

Page 29. "She fascinated me . . . of America." Andy Warhol quoted in Goldsmith, p. 99.

Page 29. "printed paintings." Andy Warhol quoted in interview with David Bourdon in ibid., p. 9.

Page 29. "Pop art is for everyone." Andy Warhol, ibid., p. 90.

Page 29. "I just paint . . . an American artist." Andy Warhol, ibid., p. 88.

Page 31. "Children were drawn . . . found it interesting." Bob Colacello quoted in a telephone interview with the author, June 27, 2005.

Page 31. "It was a constant . . . you knew dropped in." Andy Warhol quoted in Bourdon, p. 179.

Page 32. "Kids seem to like my work." Andy Warhol quoted in interview with Gretchen Berg, summer 1966, quoted in Goldsmith, p. 89.

Page 32. "Did you ever imagine . . . happens, it happens." Andy Warhol and Bess Winakor quoted in an interview in 1975, in ibid., p. 223.

REFERENCES AND RESOURCES

(*) denotes materials suitable for younger readers

BOOKS

Andy Warhol: Drawings and Illustrations of the 1950s. New York: D.A.P./
    Goliga Books, 2000.

Andy Warhol Fashion. San Francisco: Chronicle Books, 2004.

Andy Warhol Paintings for Children. Munich and New York: Prestel Publishing,
    2004.

Andy Warhol: 365 Takes. New York: Harry N. Abrams, Inc., in association with the
    Andy Warhol Museum, 2004.

Bastian, Heiner. *Andy Warhol Retrospective*. London: Tate Publishing, 2001,
    and Los Angeles: The Museum of Contemporary Art, 2002.

*Benirschke, Kurt. *Vanishing Animals: Art by Andy Warhol*. New York and Berlin:
    Springer-Verlag, 1986.

Bockris, Victor. *The Life and Death of Andy Warhol*. New York: Bantam Books,
    1989.

Bourdon, David. *Warhol*. New York: Harry N. Abrams, Inc., 1989.

Colacello, Bob. *Holy Terror: Andy Warhol Close Up*. New York: HarperCollins, 1990.

*Copplestone, Trewin. *The Life and Works of Andy Warhol*. Bristol, Great Britain:
    Parragon Book Service Ltd, 1995.

Deimling, Barbara. *Sandro Botticelli*. London: Taschen, 2000.

Dillenberger, Jane Daggett. *The Religious Art of Andy Warhol*. New York:
    The Continuum Publishing Company, 1998.

Francis, Mark and Dieter Koepplin. *Andy Warhol: Drawings 1942-1987*. Boston:
    A Bulfinch Press Book, Little, Brown and Company, 1998.

Goldsmith, Kenneth, editor. *I'll Be Your Mirror: The Selected Andy Warhol
    Interviews*. New York: Carroll & Graf Publishers, 2004.

*Greenberg, Jan & Sandra Jordan. *Andy Warhol: Prince of Pop*. New York:
    Delacorte Press, 2004.

Hackett, Pat, editor. *The Andy Warhol Diaries*. New York: Warner Books, 1989.

Honnef, Klaus. *Andy Warhol: 1928-1987*; *Commerce Into Art*. Taschen: Koln,
    Germany, 2000.

Koestenbaum, Wayne. *Andy Warhol*. New York: A Lipper/Viking Book, 2001.

*Magocsi, Paul Robert. *The Carpatho-Rusyn Americans*. New York: Chelsea
    House Publishers, 1989.

Nuland, Sherwin B. *Leonardo da Vinci*. New York: A Lipper/Viking Book, 2000.

Pop Art. Munich: Prestel Verlag, 2004.

Ratcliff, Carter. *Andy Warhol*. New York: Abbeville, 1983.

*Schaffner, Ingrid. *The Essential Andy Warhol*. New York: Harry N. Abrams, Inc.,
    1999.

Warhol, Andy. *The Philosophy of Andy Warhol (From A to B and Back Again)*
    New York: A Harvest book, Harcourt, Inc., 1975.

*Warhola, James. *Uncle Andy's*. New York: G.P. Putnam's Sons, 2003.

ARTICLES

"Carpatho-Rusyn Customs & Traditions."
Internet address: www.carpatho-rusyn.org/customs

"Carpatho-Rusyn Pysanky—Color and Beauty at Eastertime." 1990
by: GCU Honorary Editor, Michael Roman K.S.G.G.,
internet address: www.carpatho-rusyn.org/customs/gcupisan.htm

Cotter, Holland. "Everything About Warhol But the Sex." *New York Times*, Sunday,
July 14, 2002.

Hitchings, Henry. "More American Than Thinking: Andy Warhol The retrospective
Tate Modern." *TLS* February 22, 2002.

Knight, Christopher. "After the First 15 Minutes." *Los Angeles Times*, Calendar,
Sunday, May 19, 2002.

"Pop Till You Drop." Art Review by Christopher Knight. *Los Angeles Times*, Friday,
May 24, 2002.

Muchnic, Suzanne. "Selling Andy." *Los Angeles Times*, Saturday, May 4, 2002.

Vogel, Carol. "Warhol Silkscreens Bring To Prices at Auction." *New York Times*,
Friday, May 18, 2001.

LETTERS TO THE AUTHOR

James Warhola to the author via email, August 26, 2004; May 19, 2005; May 20,
2005; and May 22, 2005.

Leonard Kessler to the author October 21, 2004 and October 25, 2004.

INTERVIEWS CONDUCTED BY THE AUTHOR, VIA TELEPHONE

Leonard Kessler, August 25, 2004, and September 13, 2004.

Philip Pearlstein, May 10, 2005.

Nathan Gluck, May 12, 2005.

Tom Sokolowski, May 11, 2005, and May 16, 2005.

Matt Wrbican, July 1, 2005.

Bob Colacello, June 27, 2005.

ILLUSTRATION CREDITS

All artwork by Andy Warhol unless otherwise credited. All artworks created by Andy Warhol are © 2006 The Andy Warhol Foundation for the Visual Arts/ARS, New York.

Front cover and spine: *100 Cans*, 1962. Albright-Knox Art Gallery (details). TRADEMARKS, CAMPBELL SOUP COMPANY. ALL RIGHTS RESERVED.

Back cover: *Andy Warhol at About the Age of Eight*, 1936. The Andy Warhol Museum, Pittsburgh, Founding Collection.

Page 1: *Big Campbell's Soup Can, 19c.*, 1962. The Menil Collection, Houston. TRADEMARKS, CAMPBELL SOUP COMPANY. ALL RIGHTS RESERVED.

Page 4: *Andy Warhol with his Brother Paul*, 1942. Courtesy Paul Warhola Family.

Page 5, left: *Andy Warhol with his Mother, Julia, and his Brother John*, ca. 1930. The Andy Warhol Museum, Pittsburgh, Founding Collection. Contribution The Andy Warhol Foundation for the Visual Arts, Inc.

Page 5, right: *Andy Warhol at About the Age of Eight*, 1936. The Andy Warhol Museum, Pittsburgh, Founding Collection.

Page 6: *Dick Tracy*, 1960. Courtesy The Brandt Foundation, Greenwich, CT.

Page 7, top: *The Last Supper*, 1986. The Andy Warhol Museum, Pittsburgh, Founding Collection. Contribution The Andy Warhol Foundation for the Visual Arts, Inc. 1998.1.355

Page 7, bottom: Leonardo da Vinci. *The Last Supper*, 1494–1498. Milan, refectory of Santa Maria delle Grazie.

Page 8: *Self-Portrait*, 1942. Collection Mary Adeline McKibbin. The Andy Warhol Museum, Pittsburgh.

Page 9: *Len Kessler, Dottie Cantor and Andy Warhol*, 1948–1949. Courtesy Leonard Kessler.

Page 10: *Living Room*, ca. 1946–1947. Collection Paul Warhola Family.

Page 12: *Self-Portrait*, 1948. Collection Leonard Kessler.

Page 13, top: *Christmas Card*, 1948. Collection George Klauber Estate.

Page 13, bottom: *Andy Warhol in Manhattan*, ca. 1948–1949. Photograph by Philip Pearlstein. Courtesy Leonard Kessler.

Page 14, left: *Shoe Illustration*, from *Glamour* magazine, September 1949.

Page 14, right: "Success Is a Flying Start," from *Glamour* magazine, September 1949.

Page 15: *Lavender Sam*, from *25 Cats Named Sam and One Blue Pussy*, ca. 1955. Hand-colored photo-offset print from bound artist's book with 18 illustrations in an edition of 190, each page 9 1/8 x 6 in.

Page 16: *Butterflies*, 1955. Nathan Gluck and Luis De Jesus Collection.

Page 18: A composite of Andy Warhol's hand-colored offset prints for *A la Recherche du Shoe Perdu*, 1955. Courtesy The Andy Warhol Estate.

Page 19: Ken Heyman. *Andy Warhol at Home with his Mother*, 1966. Photograph © Ken Heyman. Courtesy Woodfin Camp Agency.

Page 20: Roy Lichtenstein. *Look Mickey*, 1961. Collection National Gallery of Art, Gift of the Artist, in Honor of the Fiftieth Anniversary of the National Gallery of Art. © 2005 Board of Trustees, National Gallery of Art, Washington. Disney characters © Disney Enterprises, Inc. Used by permission from Disney Enterprises, Inc.

Page 21: *Superman*, 1960. Collection Gunter Sachs.

Page 22: *100 Cans*, 1962. Albright-Knox Art Gallery. TRADEMARKS, CAMPBELL SOUP COMPANY. ALL RIGHTS RESERVED.

Page 23: *Big Campbell's Soup Can, 19c.*, 1962. The Menil Collection, Houston. TRADEMARKS, CAMPBELL SOUP COMPANY. ALL RIGHTS RESERVED.

Page 24, left: *Untitled (Roll of Bills)*, 1962. Courtesy The Brandt Foundation, Greenwich, CT.

Page 24, right: Andy silk-screening *Tuna Fish Disaster at the Factory*, 1963. Page 48 of *The Essential: Andy Warhol* by Ingrid Schaffner, published by Harry N. Abrams, Inc., 1999. Photo by Gerard Malanga.

Page 25: *Green Coca-Cola Bottles*, 1962. Whitney Museum of American Art, New York. Purchased with funds from Friends of the Whitney Museum of American Art. 68.25.

Page 27: *Do It Yourself (Sailboats)*, 1962. Collection Celine Heiner Bastian, Berlin, and Daros Collection, Switzerland.

Page 28: *Marilyn Monroe*, 1962. Collection Leo Castelli, New York.

Page 30: *Andy Warhol in the Factory*, 1967. Photograph © Billy Name. Courtesy Billy Name Studio.

Page 31: *Andy Warhol in the Factory*, 1967. Photograph © Billy Name/SLP Stock, New York. Courtesy Billy Name Studio.

Page 32: *Cow Wallpaper at Leo Castelli Gallery*, 1966. Courtesy Leo Castelli Gallery, New York.

Page 33: *Endangered Species: Bald Eagle (Haliatus leucocephalus)*, 1983. Courtesy Ronald Feldman Fine Arts, New York.

Page 34: *Andy Warhol*, 1986. Photograph © Christopher Makos.

Page 37: *Emergency (Helicopter)*, 1983. Courtesy Galerie Bruno Bischofberger, Zurich.

Page 40: *Moon Explorer Robot*, 1983. Courtesy Galerie Bruno Bischofberger, Zurich.

Page 42: *Andy Warhol with Children at the Opening of "Pictures for Children,"* 1983. Courtesy Galerie Bruno Bischofberger, Zurich.

AUTHOR'S NOTE

Why Warhol?

Because his art is fun. Controversial. Thought-provoking. Who else would have considered painting huge pictures of dollar bills and Coca-Cola bottles? Only Andy Warhol.

In selecting what to include in this short book, I decided to focus on Warhol's early work, his commercial art of the 1950s, and finally the paintings that established him as a Pop artist.

I decided not to talk about his experimental filmmaking. Some of his films are long and dreary. In *Empire*, a seven-hour study of the Empire State Building in New York City, almost nothing happens except that a couple of planes go by and a light is turned on.

For me Warhol's drawings and paintings are his strongest and most exciting work. He invented new ways of making pictures with multiple images that continue to influence artists to this day. Over the years his art has increased in value and is now sold at auctions for several millions of dollars.

And yet, after all this time, some people question whether Warhol's soup cans and Coke bottles are fine art. He is still the subject of controversy, which I think would have delighted him.

SOME MUSEUMS WHERE YOU WILL FIND WORK BY ANDY WARHOL

THE UNITED STATES

Birmingham Museum of Art, Birmingham, Alabama

Museum of Contemporary Art, Los Angeles, California

San Francisco Museum of Modern Art, San Francisco, California

Yale University Art Gallery, New Haven, Connecticut

Art Institute of Chicago, Chicago, Illinois

Museum of Fine Arts, Boston, Massachusetts

Detroit Institute of Arts, Detroit, Michigan

Walker Art Center, Minneapolis, Minnesota

Nelson-Atkins Museum of Art, Kansas City, Missouri

Albright-Knox Art Gallery, Buffalo, New York

Metropolitan Museum of Art, New York City

Museum of Modern Art, New York City

Whitney Museum of American Art, New York City

Ackland Art Museum at the University of North Carolina, Chapel Hill, North Carolina

Butler Institute of American Art, Youngstown, Ohio

Carnegie Museum of Art, Pittsburgh, Pennsylvania

The Andy Warhol Museum, Pittsburgh, Pennsylvania

Virginia Museum of Fine Arts, Richmond, Virginia

Modern Art Museum of Fort Worth, Fort Worth, Texas

Museum of Fine Arts, Houston, Texas

Menil Collection, Houston, Texas

National Gallery of Art, Washington, D.C.

AUSTRALIA

National Gallery of Australia, Canberra

CANADA

Art Gallery of Ontario, Toronto

National Gallery of Canada, Ottawa

Museum of Contemporary Art, Montreal, Quebec

ENGLAND

Tate Modern, London

THE NETHERLANDS

Stedelijk Museum, Amsterdam